GOD's
CHOSEN

I0132632

GOD'S
CHOSEN

BOOK 1

YULANDA CORING

Published by Beauty for Ashes

All rights reserved.
Cover design by Maria Louella Mancao
Interior design by Mary Jean Archival

Published in the United States of America

ISBN: 978-0-578-69471-9
Biography & Autobiography / Personal Memoirs
14.11.22

ACKNOWLEDGMENTS

I give honor to God first, who is Lord of my life, my best friend and whatever I need and needed him to be.

I give honor to my mother Georgia Coring next, for raising me up in holiness which made me the virtuous woman I am today, in spite of my detours, because of the way she raised me and the foundation (Jesus) placed inside of me I managed to get back on track.

I give honor to my spiritual father Pastor Fred Gamble and his lovely wife Patricia Gamble for being there for me the times I needed someone to pray for me, and pray me through hard times, and also people who follow God with their whole heart as exemplified in Psalm 37:37, "Mark the perfect man, and behold the upright: for the end of that man is peace," ever since God allowed them to be a part of my life.

PART 1

Ever since I was a little girl growing up I have experienced loneliness. I remember when I was still a little girl under thirteen, how I would be outside on our porch playing with a mop turned upside down and pretending that I was on those soap operas. I did not really know how to make friends. I was what people called shy and bashful. I played most of the time with my brothers and sisters or my cousins who lived close by, or alone. My mother was, and still is, a Christian and she did the things she knew how to do to show us she loved us such as: feeding, clothing, and taking care of us, and sending and taking us to church on Sunday. Even though she sometimes mentioned the reason why she never really told us she loved us when we were growing up was, because her mother never really told her. She stated that is why she did not know how to tell us, but I guess I never really put a lot of thought into it, because I feel that she showed us by being there raising us and not leaving us when my father did countless times. I feel that she did the best she could under the circumstances and pressure she was put under by my father. My father not being there for me is one of the reasons why I sometimes feel alone and have resentment toward some things. Even now as an adult, I sometimes cry when I think about the way we were treated by my father.

On one occasion as a little girl, I can remember my older sisters, brothers and I having to steal money out of my father's pants' pockets while he was taking a shower, because he had stopped giving my mother money, because he had several other women. My mom never told us to do it; we did it because we needed money. One day he realized what we were doing and addressed my mom and us concerning it and threatened us with trouble if he caught us doing it. I can recall other times while I was still a child under thirteen years old that I remember my dad abusing my mom. One time was when my parents were standing in the kitchen. I am not sure of the exact location where I was standing at that time, but I know it had to have been very close to them because I saw everything. All I remember is my mom fixing my dad some cereal and my dad getting the cereal and throwing it in my mom's face. Then when she reached down to pick the cereal up off the floor along with the spoon, he kicked her out of the kitchen, into the utility room. I don't remember exactly what happened after that probably because I ran and hid, because that is what me, my brothers, and sisters used to do when that happened to Mom. Another time concerning abuse that I remember was when Mom was ironing my father's wet pair of pants because he wanted them ironed dry, so he made her iron them dry. I can remember him snatching the iron from her and threatening to burn her with the iron holding it up in her face. I remember her backing up and pleading with him and crying. She was pregnant with my baby brother at that time. He continued to walk towards her and she continued backing up until she backed into the kitchen counter and slipped down on the floor, and I believe that God allowed her to fall because that is what caused him to walk away from her and not burn her. I am assuming my father then put on his street clothing and then went out on the street where his other women were, including some people very close to my mom, but that is another story. I can remember him backing off the porch several times while I would be pretending like I was on *Days of Our Lives* acting with a mop turned upside down. I would watch him back off the porch and I would be wishing that he would spend time with me. I had a friend around my age and she would tell me how her Father taught her how to drive and would let her drive his car. I would watch my father leave in his car and wish that he would teach me how to drive. He never taught my mother how to drive, so I should have known that it was not going to happen for me. I felt really sad and alone because I was too young to realize that God was there for me even thought my father had forsaken me. We were not even allowed near my father's three vehicles, much less in them. My Mom could not ride in them either. He only rode his other women and their children around in his vehicles. The reason my mom stayed with him is because he always threatened to find her and kill her if she left. I believe he would have done just that, because he murdered an innocent, intoxicated man who wandered up to the wrong door, which was our door, thinking it was someone else's door. My dad automatically assumed that he was there for my mom, and shot and killed him. My oldest brother would have nightmares about it. My father only did a week in jail due to some involvement his mother had, but that is another story. Other times I can remember as a child, my father putting all of us outside at night sometimes when he did stay at home. My mom and us kids would wait until he fell asleep, then my mom would send my smallest brother at that time to go and climb in the bathroom window and unlock the door so we could come back in. I guess my childhood was more of a nightmare than a childhood because everything seemed like something that happens in nightmares, not in real life. I remember on one night we were put out on the porch and a guy that liked one of my older sisters rode by our house on a bicycle, and he yelled up there on our porch,

"Theresa, is that you?" Then my father opened the door and cursed him out then the guy sped off on the bicycle. Then my father closed the door and left us out there if I am not mistaken. My father was not completely bad because he used to give my mom money and provide for us on certain occasions such as Christmas, etc. until he got involved with some woman who dealt in witchcraft and practiced it on him. It prospered against him because he was not a Christian, and also not covered by the blood of Jesus. I can recall times as a child in church, people prophesying to my mom and telling her that women have worked witchcraft on my dad, and letting her know that that is one of the reasons why he was treating her like he was.

Another reason why my father treated my mother the way he did was because he was not originally meant to be her husband. He was not sent to her by God. I also recall people prophesying and informing her that women were attempting to work witchcraft on her, but it did not prosper, because she was in and is still in God (a Christian). Even though my mother never told us she loved us verbally, she expressed it spiritually in addition to financially. The only life I recall my mother having is a life that revolved around God. I recall her just about every day on her room floor praying and crying out to God, and interceding for us as well. I also recall her raising us up on only Gospel music, such as Shirley Caesar, All Green, etc. We were not allowed to listen to worldly music, but we sometimes did it unknown to her. I also recall her taking us to church every Sunday and sometimes on week nights, especially if revivals came in town. God, through her instilled morals in us, such as teaching us to do right and not wrong; for example, not to lie, steal (God's Commandments). I am not implying that my mom was perfect, because no one is, but only stating that God in her trained us up the right way, even though we did not always do completely right. So we might have detoured a few times, but we didn't completely depart from the foundation that was and is still placed in us. Even though my mother was a righteous and godly woman, she and I never established a mother-daughter bond for some reason. I always felt as a child that I was adopted. She never treated me bad, but I guess I felt that way because she and I never formed a bond or made a connection, just like me and my father never did. I grew up feeling always alone and also shy and feeling different. I felt that I didn't fit in with people even though I would talk with them and acknowledge them as a friend. I would sometimes wonder why I could not act like them, or be loud like them or bold like them. I did not realize then, that I was one of God's chosen people, and that is why I could never fit in and be like others. I was one of his peculiar people and did not know it at that time. Even though I was raised in church, I never accepted Christ into my life as a child, so I really did not know much about being chosen by God. I am sure they preached about it in my old childhood church, but obviously I did not grasp the concept of it as a child. As I got older, like an older teenager or young adult, I can recall different prophets coming through our church and having revivals. God, through some of them, would prophesy to me. They would tell me, "You are chosen from your mom's womb." It meant that God chose me from my mother's womb, which includes being appointed and anointed by God, and also includes being separated from the world (which is stated in John 15). The purpose for being chosen by God is to minister the Gospel to people to encourage them to accept God into their lives, and also for God in us to perform miracles, etc., so he will be glorified, because he made us for his purpose and use. Even though it was told to me that I was chosen I still could not do the spiritual work that God wanted me to do because I was not a Christian then, and it would have been like the blind leading the blind.

I, witnessing my father abusing my mother, continued up until I was thirteen years old. One night he decided to put us out while my mother was at work doing an eleven-to-seven shift. I vaguely remember the exact reason but I recall bits and pieces, such as him wanting one of my sisters to iron his pants dry. Then I recall another sister shouting and telling him, "Leave my sister alone!" Then I recall him slapping her. He ended up putting us out that night as well. My mother was called at her job by the police to come and get us. She left her job and came and got us and asked us why we didn't go back in through the bathroom window. We told her we tried but the window was locked. She took us to my eldest sister's apartment then went back to work. She stated she cried at work concerning the situation for two hours.

We stayed at my sister's place for about a month then my mom managed to get her own apartment. We moved there and stayed there a few days without lights. While we were there my father attempted to get my mother to move back in our old home. My mother refused to move back with him, so he threatened to sell our home and he did.

Soon after that my father became ill and was diagnosed with cirrhosis of the liver. He got down really sick and lost a lot of weight and had to be hospitalized with a variety of tubes placed in him. It was prophesied to my mother in church that if she had not prayed for my father, he would have died. After my father was released he asked my mom if he could come live with her but she refused. My grandmother then came down from out of town and took him back with her. Before he completely recovered from his sickness he lost his mind and could not remember my mom when she went to visit him. His mind was later restored. Months later when we were still living in the same place, the rent started to become a challenge for my mom to pay. Especially when one of my sisters went off to college and left only one of my sisters there to help my mom manage the bills. After Mom realized that she could no longer afford to pay all of the bills with just help from only one of my sisters, she decided to apply for low income housing by adding her name on a waiting list. She stated that God had placed that in her spirit before to put her name on that list, but she did not obey him and ignored it, because she was still with my father. Soon after she applied for the housing, she got accepted and we moved there. It was not as bad as I thought it would be considering that it was a low income apartment in a not so good area. Then we moved to a quiet and nice apartment located in a good area.

I had become a teenager about sixteen years old. The only thing that really changed in my life is that I started to hang out with my cousin and with a group of friends, which was something I never was allowed to do or used to do when my mother was with my father. I also got in fights I never started, and would pull and carry knives and have even stabbed some people, but that did not just start then. I was doing that at about the age of twelve.

On one occasion when I was twelve, I recall my grabbing one of my mother's butcher knives and chasing a group of girls away that were standing in front of my parents' house bothering me. After I chased them away I then targeted one of them that I really did not like and almost stabbed her, and would have if a guy wouldn't have grabbed me by my shirt. I had previously beaten her up in our ditch. So, as I stated earlier, pulling and utilizing knives did not just start, but hanging out did. I can remember me mainly hanging out with my female cousin. We were very close and would attempt to double date. I also recall going to block parties with the group of girls I hung out with. I am not calling them or my cousin bad influences because I had a mind of my own, but I just think that if I wouldn't have been hanging out at all, I would not have lost my virginity when I was a late teenager. I think as a teenager I really was not happy and not motivated. I am sure it was due to what I had already experienced as a child. Even in school I know I would have done a lot better and worked a lot harder if I had only had a parent, sibling, or someone to motivate and encourage me. That is why I constantly motivate and encourage my kids today. On another occasion as a teenager, I can recall being involved with this guy in college when he came home for the summer. I think that was my first true love. I recall me running up my mom's phone bill and other family member's and loved one's phone bills just to talk to him when he was out of state in college. I remember one night I went to his house when he was down but he was not home so I decided to climb in through the back window and wait in an empty room. When he came home, I heard a female's voice as well, so I moved something around in the room to make some noise. After that he came walking down the hall with a gun and entered the room. It was dark in the room but thank God he did not shoot before he looked to see who it was. So God spared my life again. After he asked how I got in there, he escorted me out the door. I was very upset so

I went to one of my friend's grandmother's house and asked if I could borrow her knife to get a piece of gum off of my shoe. After she gave it to me, I took off back to his house and stabbed one of his tires. It made a lot of noise so I ran. He came to my mom's home and told her while I was standing at the window looking at him.

As I stated earlier, I also hung out with my cousin. I recall another event when she and I were out double dating two brothers. We all were driving over a bridge and somehow the eldest brother lost control of the steering wheel in the middle of the bridge which did not have any railing. We almost went off the bridge but God took control of the steering wheel and allowed the driver to regain control. Again, God spared my life and had his hand on me. It was a very frightening experience. After that we continued to hang out and I continued to get into fights and arguments but never really started them. I thank God that consequences from carrying and using knives in my days were not as serious as they are these days. I tell my kids that all the time.

In my days, I never got in trouble for stabbing people, except on one occasion when I was eighteen, an adult. I almost did, but God blocked it that time as well. It started when I was in my seventh period class and this boy that liked me came in there to see the teacher. The boy took it upon himself to start playing with me and pulling the back of my hair. I think I told him to stop because it was hurting but he proceeded to do it. So I got my pencil and I started stabbing him in the hand. I think the teacher made him leave the class. But before he left he threatened to get me after school. So after my cousin and I got off the bus we started walking to my house which was about half a mile away from the bus stop. My cousin was pregnant at that time. As we walked on, the same boy had another boy drive him by us while we were walking. He got out of the car, grabbed me, and threw me down on the ground. My cousin asked him to leave me alone but he did not. After he threw me down I bumped my head on the road and got a large knot on the side of it. Then he got back in the car and they drove away. I walked or ran to my mom's house and grabbed a knife. I did not tell her anything but my cousin did. After I grabbed the knife, I ran all the way down to the store where he and all the rest of the guys would hang out. I met him in the store. He was at the counter. I stabbed him in the chest and then he grabbed me and threw me behind the counter. By then my mom had called my uncle and the police, and a lot of other people were present. So the police arrested him and had him standing on the outside, I guess 'cause I stabbed him. They put me in the back of a police car. He was outside but I was not. While they were busy doing whatever they were doing, I managed to get out of the police car while it had the police locks on it. How I know it was locked on the inside is because they asked how I got out later on. Anyway, when I did get out I escaped them all without any of them even noticing me. I went right across to my sister's house and got one of her knives unknown to her. I then went back to the scene and attempted to stab the guy again while he was handcuffed right in front of the police. One of the officers then pulled his gun from his holster and had it aimed at me and told me to drop the knife or he would shoot. So I dropped the knife and they handcuffed me that time. After they hauled both of us off to jail because one of the officers who did not care too much for my family was already chanting and thinking I was going to jail, so he said. They then placed both of us in holding cells. After hours passed, a guard came to my cell and stated to me that I was being released because the guy had dropped the charges. So obviously God's plans for me were not to go to prison and have a record. He had better plans for my life.

The last major event I can recall happening, before I graduated and left our low income housing, was when my baby brother got run over while riding his bicycle by a long station wagon. He was somewhere between six and nine years old. It happened in front of the same store where the majority of the events that happened with me and that guy took place. To my understanding he was riding his bicycle behind this huge station wagon and the girl did not see him and backed over him. I was told that he was completely under the vehicle. He died at the scene but after a Christian woman prayed for him, God brought him back to life. He ended up in pretty bad condition with pins and screws in his skull and also losing his mind, but before he became an adult, God restored it. It was prophesied to my mom that it would be restored before he turned eighteen. He received something else good from this event besides God bringing him back to life. He also met Princess Diana and took pictures with her at the Children's Hospital while he was being treated. That was the last serious event I recall happening before I left my home town.

After I graduated I decided not to go to college right away but to go off to Atlanta with a close friend from the group at that time. After I got there, I realized it had not been a wise decision. I ended up messing up my credit by making bad choices. We worked three jobs and that was basically it. I really did not like being around large crowds at parties and crab boils. I would mainly stay upstairs. I guess it's because I was chosen by God and different. I was a shy and quiet person the way God made me. So people thought I was different, and I was, and I still am one of God's peculiar people. That lasted only for a while then we moved to Florida. Then I moved an hour away from my home town to a place called Fort Myers. I stayed with my aunt and cousins. It was a unique experience as well. The cousins who I grew up with were not really close there as we had been as kids. I really did not feel welcome there either, but that is another story. Later, I met my first child's father and months after that we conceived my daughter. He was not truthful to me really about anything. I was still young, about nineteen, so when I did some investigating inside his car and found little secrets, he would just tell me that it was really this and not what I thought. So after I became pregnant I found out he was really married and everything else came to the light. By then it was too late to leave him alone, so I thought. I ended up moving back home for some months until I had my daughter. After I had her I went into a shelter so I could be in the same city with her father and so they could help me get an apartment, which they did. So soon after I moved into the shelter I got a job, then God blessed me to get an apartment. So my daughter and I moved in our own apartment. It was a low income apartment but it was pretty decent aside from the guys that hung outside of it urinating in the elevators and stairways. My daughter's father would come over at times. He also would stalk me and sit out under my apartment. I knew this because he would mention that I kept my lights on all night, and I never told him that.

I still would fight as an adult but not as much as I did as a child. I recall one specific conflict with me and my daughter's father's wife. We had a fist fight and I started turning my arms like a windmill really fast with my fist balled up. We called that type of fighting when I was growing up "the wild Cathy" which was named after a girl named Cathy that fought wild in my neighborhood. I was swinging really fast until I ended up ripping her shirt off causing her to walk away from the store without a shirt or bra on. I was originally only supposed to meet him there but she followed him. She and I continued to have arguments thereafter. I attempted to go back to Atlanta for a little while to save money, but because of opposition that did not work either. While I was up there my apartment in Florida got broken into. I heard that the neighbors played a part in it. Then I heard it was other people retaliating but that is another story, as well. So, I returned from Atlanta and got a job and attempted to get established. I ended up having to return the vehicle I got from Atlanta due to it being obtained the wrong way with the help of friends. So I decided at that time to work for a daycare but ended up walking out because of lack of interest. The dating game was also not going too well because I guess I had not met the right guy yet, and having my daughter's father come in and out of my life. I tried to do housekeeping but that was entirely too hard, so I thought.

PART 2

I guess I was at that stage where I really did not know what I wanted to do with my life, but I knew for sure becoming a Christian was not on my list then, because I was still deep in sin and whoremongering. So for whatever reason, I guess because I always knew how to dance as a child and as an adult, I developed a thought in my head that I was going to start dancing. I guess I was just thinking about making money until I really did not think about the way I was raised, such as with morals and with my mom raising us up in holiness. At first a girl and I were both going to do it, but she backed out because of her jealous boyfriend. So I developed boldness from wherever and went to apply and try out by myself.

After I got in there, I started dancing every weekend. I can recall having to get tipsy with alcohol before I went on stage. My stage name was Foxy Brown but for some reason when the African-American guys started to hang out there, they would call me what the club was named, Paradise. Every time I went on stage I felt degraded. I guess because I still had the foundation that my mom instilled inside of me, the foundation meaning, God. I know that is why I felt degraded and uncomfortable doing it. It brought a lot of attention to me and I made more money there than I had ever made anywhere else just working on weekends. In spite of all of that I still hated it. After I continued to do it for a while, I soon met my now ex-husband there.

We started talking at first then eventually started dating. I was glad when I met him and we started dating seriously and he moved in, so I did not have to dance any longer and he did not want me to either. So I was grateful for that. I do not think my mom found out about it, but I know I told one of my sisters. I went back maybe a few times after he and I moved in together, but then I finally let it go. For me it was a degrading experience with a lot of indecent things taking place there, but it was still a choice I made at that time to make a living. So he and I moved in together and started our new relationship. Early in our relationship everything seemed almost perfect. I was treated like a queen. He never argued with me or went against me, and whatever I asked him to do, he did it. I should have realized then that it was too good to be true. I even would let him babysit my daughter at times when I ran errands. It is like I could not believe how easygoing he was, so sometimes I would slap him in the face just to see his response which was nothing. Yeah, I should have known better. While we were still in our early stages of dating, I found out I was pregnant from my daughter's father whom I was involved with before I met my husband. I did not want any more kids from my daughter's father so I decided to get an abortion which was another bad choice. I asked my boyfriend at the time, now my ex-husband, if he could pay for it and he agreed, but I knew it was not comfortable for him or for me. I did the abortion which was the first of the multiple abortions. It was not a pleasant experience especially when the doctor asked you a variety of questions such as: are you sure you want to terminate the pregnancy? Then the other sad things that followed. But I just felt at that time that I did not want to have another child from him when he was not really taking good care of my daughter, and our relationship was really based on lies and deceit because of his untruthfulness. After I managed to get over the abortion, which I really do not think I ever completely erased it from my mind, I probably just numbed myself to the pain along with the other pain that had accumulated from childhood; I continued moving on with my life so what I thought was going to finally be a happy life. Things were still continuing to go swell, and a few months into our relationship, I ended up getting pregnant by him. I pretty soon realized I was very fertile. Things were good up until one day about seven or eight months into the pregnancy, we were driving down the highway. I am not sure what we were arguing about, but I think it was something dealing with his past relationship, that it was over. I remember that I placed my hand on the gear shift and threatened to force the car out of gear. He then hit my hand really hard. I do not recall what happened after that, but that was the beginning of me being abused. On another occasion I can recall us having an argument and somehow he pushed me down on the floor. I was still pregnant at that time. I called the police and had him arrested, but the next day I went and told the judge he did not do it, because I know he had to go back to work since I was not working at that time. Soon after that, I had my son, and it seemed like after that the arguing and fighting increased. I felt that maybe he felt he had me trapped after I ended up getting pregnant from him. So my dreams of having a functional and happy family, something I never had as a child, were shattered. The fighting increased and intensified as time went on. He was a halfway decent father to our son and my daughter (his stepdaughter). He provided for them and me financially and we also did family things together such as going out to dinner, have barbecues, etc. He had good things about him but he also had negative things, which outweighed the good such as cursing and saying really bad and nasty words to me in front of my kids and calling me outside of my name which provokes me to grabbing knives and stabbing him. He knew how to make someone feel really small when he said bad things. There was a lot of verbal and physical abuse involved. A lot of times it was from him calling me bad names and me retaliating by calling him names back, resorting him to put his hands on me, physically abusing me. I can recall one occasion where we were fighting in the kitchen and food ended up everywhere.

My kids would always go and jump behind the couch in the living room. I remember our fights being so crazy until sometimes the devil would make me or him do extremely crazy things. One specific occasion, we got in a verbal fight, then physical fight, and I stabbed him in the arm. After I stabbed him, he poured the blood from his arm all over my clothes. Why he did it I am not sure, and the only reason I could think of is to mess up my clothing because I would always by expensive clothing. On another occasion I can recall us getting into a verbal and physical fight and him getting up in my face speaking negative things and spit accidently flying in my face. I purposely spit in his face then he spat back in mine and I am assuming that probably continued. I remember having to go to the emergency room once because he sprained my wrist twisting it while he was trying to take a knife out of my hand. I remember on different occasions when he went to the emergency room to get stitches for stab wounds, and I would be at home afraid and waiting, and thinking that he was going to tell the doctor and police the truth that time, but he never did. He stated they would ask him want happened but he never responded. That was just God having and keeping his hand on me just like all the other times. Our relationship grew more and more miserable. We argued like cats and dogs daily with my kids witnessing it as I did as a child. My kids would sometimes cry, but the majority of the time they would run and hide mainly behind the sofa. It seemed like our fighting soon became common to them until I think that they soon thought of it as being a game because they would jump behind the sofa and then sometimes peep their heads up and down, then run to other hiding areas.

I then started nursing school then ended up having to stop then restart because of my son's outpatient surgery. After I restarted I managed to stay afloat in spite of the daily fighting. I can recall one incident when I obtained a scratch on my left arm from fighting. One of my instructors noticed and asked me what happened because they were already aware of me being in an abusive relationship. I told her that I bruised easily. Then she looked at me like she did not believe me. My ex-husband and I continued to fight throughout nursing school, causing me to become more nervous.

Nervousness was an issue for me since childhood. I guess I really expressed my nervousness while attending nursing school because the instructors were strict and also observant, and aware of my being abused, and that was something that I really did not want to cause an episode report to be done. There was really no way to hide scars. I was late a lot and nervous, etc., when being observed performing various techniques. In spite of those issues and the instructors being aware of things, I still managed to stay afloat and function like the others. Then after finally making it to the third semester, after the majority of the class and I had to redo the second semester due to the instructor testing on material not assigned, I ended up entering into what seemed like hell instead of third semester. The reason I am saying this is because I was receiving pure hell. Others were treated badly also but it just seemed like I was her bull's-eye. God's discernment had let me know when I first saw this lady in first semester and she gave me a hard time, it revealed to me that I was going to have issues with her when I got to the third semester, and I did. During the semester this lady was a nightmare to everyone but mainly to me. It is like every time we were on clinicals in the hospital and she came on the floor, everyone hid inside of a room. It is like she tormented me more than others and it was because I was chosen by God, which means that I was selected to be picked on. My test and trials did not just start when I became a Christian, but ever since I was a little girl. So while I was in the third semester this lady gave me such a hard time, until it got to the point where I became completely paralyzed when I had to perform a procedure while I was with her. So the head instructor placed me with another one temporarily. She was firm but she was fair, unlike the other one. So while I was with her I was able to function again. One of my classmates was a Christian and she was from the same place as me. Her family knew my family well. She brought me a bible and told me that her father wanted me to read Mark 11:22–26, which states about a mountain being removed. Her family also came out to talk to the lady and also to pray. While in almost the last part of the semester and school year, I ended up back with the instructor that gave me hell, because we were going into a subject that only she taught (obstetrics). Nothing changed from the first time I was with her and if anything, matters got worse. In spite of her giving me a hard time I still managed to stay afloat and passed tests. I think that is what she did not like. I am assuming when she realized that she could not fail me in my grades or get me kicked out of school as she attempted to earlier, she went to plan C which was failing me in one of the procedures we had to physically perform, which was a neonatal assessment. She did not check me off on it because she stated I did not do it right when I know I studied the procedure very well. So she managed to fail me in that, causing me to come back a month after graduation just to meet her in the hospital to redo that procedure before I could complete the semester. So after she failed me and told me I would have to come back, we started preparing for finals toward the end of school. I had gotten so depressed and stressed out, until I could not and did not study for my

OB final. I just knew I was going to fail it, because I did not study and I had given up and only wanted to lay in bed and not study. Then God came through for me once again and I managed to get a "C" on the final even though I did not study for it. God led me to study all the other prior small tests really well, and he helped me because he saw that I put my best in the small test so that is why he did the rest. Like I always tell myself and my kids, "Do your best and God will do the rest." So making a long story short, after I came back after graduation just to perform the neonatal assessment, she pretended that I performed it extremely well. I thought to myself that this was the same way I performed it the first time.

Anyway, after that followed IV (intravenous) therapy which was taught by her and other instructors, but she really did not have any involvement with me which was good. I guess she realized it was over. I did not invite my husband at that time to my graduation because I felt he did not deserve to come because of all the things he put me through. I was still a sinner at that time so I thought that was what he deserved. I let him stay home and babysit my kids which he ended up becoming very familiar with because of all of our arguing and fighting.

After completing the entirety of nursing and IV therapy, I took the state Board of Nursing exam and managed with God's help to pass it on the first attempt. It was half hard and half easy, and I felt that I had done really bad that they shut me off at eighty-five questions and did not want me to continue, but instead it meant that I did good. After receiving my nursing license, I began working as a nurse, working at various places and working various shifts. The arguing and fighting between me and my significant other which became my husband in 2003, two years after I graduated in 2001, did not cease. In fact our marriage really began to plummet because of our fighting which caused and provoked me to start hanging out with friends and partying and drinking, because I had a retaliative spirit and refused to be controlled due to me watching my mom being controlled. Whenever we got into a fight I would leave out of the house and leave him babysitting on purpose. Sometimes I met resistance leaving out of the house and sometimes I could not leave due to him standing in the way or taking the keys. The times I did manage to get out of the house which was more than less, I would go and date other people only to retaliate, because of him calling me out my name and fighting me. Our relationship was in such turmoil until I ended up getting pregnant from him and having multiple abortions but under six, because I really did not want to bring any more kids into a dysfunctional situation. Each time was really emotional, painful, and sad for me and him as well, and the same questions asked over again each time for the abortion. The doctor did not make anything easier. It just seemed at that time that it was the best decision because we had attempted therapy and other interventions without success. The time frame the abortions took place was between 2001 to the end of 2004 before November.

After looking for love in all the wrong places because of provocation, I finally ended up getting tired of the world, which was really the case as soon as I first started. I ended up one day getting on my knees in my bedroom and asking God for forgiveness for sinning against him and for his salvation and receiving them both in addition to inviting him in my heart. After becoming a born again Christian, I felt much better about myself and started observing life from a Christian stand point. Even though I became a Christian, my husband did not follow, but the physical abuse did stop and only the verbal and mental abuse remained. He would when asked to go to church, engage in bible study, and pray with me and our kids. Besides the abuse, he was not really a bad man and I am not sure if he ever cheated, just only sometimes he would be observed having unfaithful eyes and when confronted he did not acknowledge it. After about a year of continuing to put up with his verbal abuse and having to be a humble Christian, I decided to consider filing for divorce. After the divorce was filed he asked if that was what I wanted and I stated yes with lots of sadness in my heart. Even though I really did not want to go through with it, I realized that there were not going to be any changes going forth in him for the better because of pride, and not willing to change his ways even though I changed mine. I believed

God could have changed him, but only if he wanted and allowed God to do it and dropped his pride.

So the way I saw it was either I get a divorce, or go back into the world and start hanging out and cussing him back when it was done to me. The divorce process was painful and grievous for us both and for our kids, and the three months it took for it to be finalized seemed like a year instead. My ex-husband asked if that was what I really wanted and after much thought, I said yes. I felt in my spirit that he did not really want to get the divorce and God also revealed to me in a dream that he was sitting in a chair looking really sad. Even though I was kind of reluctant to get the divorce also, I realized it was really the only option because he was not going to change or allow God to change him because of the proud heart he walked around with. I realized that we would never be able to walk together if we were not in agreement with each other, as the Bible states. After the divorce was finalized I decided, after praying myself and having my spiritual father pray, to move to Louisiana. I was at first torn between Louisiana and Texas because I knew a Christian friend who lived in Louisiana, and I had a sister who lived in Texas at the time. God through my spiritual father got back with me after he prayed and told me that it was okay for me to move to Louisiana, he did not mention anything about Texas, so obviously Louisiana was where God was leading me for whatever reasons. I also received confirmation from another older man of God when I had moved to Louisiana, stating that I made the right move. He stated it on two different occasions in church. So my two kids and I, with the assistance of my ex-husband, packed up and moved to Louisiana. We donated a lot of things we could not take with us to the local Salvation Army.

When we arrived there in Louisiana God had already opened up a door and provided us with a great and safe place to stay. Without me having a job, I guess you could say I moved to Louisiana by faith. About a week later he opened up a door for a job. Everything pretty much fell into place before and after I moved up there, because it was God's will. My kids later got into magnet schools similar to those they had attended in Florida. I then attempted to go to Oral Roberts University by correspondence until opposition from the enemy started. It first started or I guess I should say the devil first started when I placed my son in a private school before he got accepted in a magnet school. I placed him in a private school when he was in fourth grade. My purpose for removing him from a public school and placing him in a private school was because of the unsuccessful passing rate of the Louisiana Educational Assessment Program Test also known as the LEAP in spite of him getting good grades. I felt in my heart that I wasn't about to allow my son to be set up for failure he did not deserve, because he had passing grades but not enough LEAP preparation from the school. After he entered private school, opposition arose. The teacher at first seemed like she was not really interested in my son's success or the other kid's success also. She would continuously give my son Fs on pretty much every assignment. When I attempted to talk to her, she would have a chip on her shoulder and nothing at first got accomplished. It caused me to have to withdraw from Oral Roberts University by correspondence and focus entirely on helping my son study for just about everything in his books that we possibly thought would be on the test. I prayed and cried out to God and asked him to not let my son fail in spite of what the enemy was trying to do. My son and I labored and stayed up studying until two or three in the morning, then we would get up early in the morning and study even on the way to school. I felt that the enemy had gotten so busy in this woman that my son and I literally had to give up anything else besides studying. And I was crying out to God. One day somehow this woman and I got into a conversation about her personal life which was unrelated to my son's schooling. It was like she confided in me because she knew I was a Christian. God, through me, also ministered to her. We then began to develop something like a friendship and shared personal stories concerning our lives. Then after that, she would inform my son and me of what areas in the book to study. She did not give us any test answers and as a Christian I did not expect her to do that. She was only then doing what she should have done for my son and for the other children in the beginning. Long story made short, because of prayer first and then me showing kindness, in spite of the torture my son and I were going through, God softened her heart and allowed her to help my son and he managed to finish the fourth grade on the honor roll. Other kids, close to half, were not that blessed and did not even make it to the next grade, sad to say.

After that hard test and trial allowed by God, the devil decided to take things up to higher levels. Allowed once again by God, he decided to affect and afflict me emotionally, and that is exactly what he did. Right before the devil started, my older cousin who is a prophet, prophesied to me and told me that the devil was trying to take me out emotionally, and right after that it started. The platonic friends I knew in Louisiana switched out on me and turned their backs leaving me and my kids without family or friends. I then cried out to God concerning that, and also concerning my family in Florida (my mom, etc.) because my family had turned against me as well. In other words the devil was trying to make me his bull's-eye and take me out whatever way he could, because I am chosen by God and have a special calling and anointing on my life. One day in 2010 I called this Christian man who knew my family. I called him for prayer. This man was also a prophet, and as I stated earlier, I was raised in a prophetic atmosphere where God, through people, operated in those gifts. God through me have those supernatural, prophetic gifts as well.

PART 3

Anyway this prophet prayed for me and after praying, God led him to send me to an old friend of his that he had known for ten years and who lived here in Louisiana, and who was also a pastor and prophet. I thought God, through this prophet, was sending me to this man and his church because I had just left another church and my kids and I needed a new church home. But when I got to the church and joined, I was introduced to the pastor/prophet. About three months later God started revealing to me that this pastor/prophet was meant to be my husband. God would show me in dreams about him attempting to propose to me, but in the dreams it seemed like when he tried to propose to me something nasty like a body part would come between us. Like for instance, it was indicating that, because he was sleeping around and not in the right place with God, that is what was preventing us from becoming married. Also there would be women, two main and obvious ones, sitting on the front pews, one on each side. When I came he obviously picked up spiritually that I was meant to be his wife and would sometimes throw hints in the air about a husband and a wife and taking the wife out to dinner and other hints to let me know that he knew. Obviously the two main women picked things up as well and began to hate on me, stare at me, try to sit in front of me so he could not see me. Even on one occasion they try to knock me down without success, but thank God for him residing in me and not the old man. One even tried to call herself, lay her hands on my head and pray for me but, of course, I caught her hand with my hand and did not allow her to lay her hand on my head. The Bible states the blind cannot lead the blind, so what I am saying is, of course, the blind cannot lead the righteous. Our God ordained marriage that never took place physically and was only just spiritual dealings continued on just being spiritual things, because he rejected God's way due to him being in the flesh (darkness) and not in the Holy Spirit (light). I think the problem was he raised himself up above God and he preferred to not come out of darkness/bondage, and surrender to God's will, and obey him and marry me. The Bible states in John 3:19 that men love darkness rather than light because their deeds were evil. He appeared to me as having half good ways and half bad ways.

The good ways would have been when he would mention marriage and sometimes look at me, and throw other hints that I knew would be referring to me. The bad ways were he would sometimes send out spirits by the spirit to afflict me with headaches, and also send out hindering spirits and tormenting spirits. God would reveal them to me and also reveal to me that the man was jealous of my anointing; God let me know it was like a Saul and David thing from the Bible. For example Saul in the Bible was jealous of David because Saul only killed one thousand people in war while David killed ten thousand.

It was prophesied to me by a woman that someone attempted to kill me by witchcraft but could not because I had God's grace. God revealed to me that it was him. I forgave and continued to go to that church, until God let me know otherwise not to, because I was always told if God sent you to a church, you have to let him uproot you from there and send you elsewhere. As I stated I continued to go there but I also visited this other church that I go to whenever I felt the pain was becoming unbearable to keep taking at this church. I can recall feeling that my mind was almost being pushed out of my head like the devil was trying to still it by making me think about the abuse I suffered mentally, and sometimes verbally when he would lie and speak out to the audience and tell them that when some people praise and worship and they would be faking, he would be throwing hits at me. How he made me suffer mentally and spiritually is by mentioning things about a husband and a wife like he was going to do the right thing but never did. My old pastor and my cousin, through each one of them, told me they saw me getting married, in addition to God letting me know, but because the man refused to come out of darkness and into God's marvelous light, it never happened. I stayed there at that church for nine months going through torture and being tricked, played with, and fooled. It bothered my mind so much because even though it was God's will for us, they would not comply with God and remain keeping it a spiritual relationship versus bringing it out in the light because they were walking in darkness. So I ended up leaving. Right before I left, they did some type of stage play about getting married, but I assumed that it was another hoax.

After I left, I had a dream that I was leaving their church, which I had already done, and they did not want me to leave. So I guess God was letting me know my time was up there, but I had already left days before I had the dream. So my kids and I joined this other church. The pastor was young, around my age. The pastor of the church that I left was in his fifties. God did not really show me anything about him, but the thing I would sometimes think is that he was the ram in the bush like in the Bible. In other words, he was the spare man. God did not show me that but he let me know that he would flip it for me and this guy, meaning even though he is not the original (the Isaac). God could flip things and turn them around since God had already promised me my desires. God even showed in a dream that he would and was able to flip it. The guy also could see in the spirit like me and he seemed pretty true like a true pastor, but he eventually married someone else, hurting me again. I never came on to him or expressed that I was interested in him, but because he could see in the spirit realm he picked my thoughts and sometimes would make me think that he was going to be the ram in the bush like God would have flipped it, but he eventually married someone else. So after he announced that he was getting married to someone else, I felt that there was no other reason for me to stay there, so my kids and I eventually left. In addition to all of this, I was receiving persecutions at my job also. People were lying about me, laughing at me, talked about me and the enemy made several attempts to get me fired. It was a negative charge nurse at my job that was continuously trying to get me fired for about three years, but God gave me favor with my director of nursing and it never prospered. Also I ended up getting a perfect evaluation by my director of nursing. Soon after my director of nursing left that job and went to another, that negative charge nurse attempted to get me fired again. She went to the new administrator and told a bunch of lies on me and, being the administrator was new, he believed her as she was the charge nurse. So obviously, if God allowed me to get fired this time and never the other times, then my time was up there. I then filed for unemployment and, through God, beat the unemployed case. The judge was completely in agreement with me and not the charge nurse or the administrator because God, through the judge, saw that I was innocent. It was not really a big deal about me losing my job at that time because my kids and I were living with a roommate at that time, and I was paying my half of the rent out of my child support. The only thing that got behind was my car payment because I lost my job in January 2011 and I did not get money from unemployment until May 2011. My income tax also ended up getting taken because of student loans, so it was really in that year, 2011, that I had one test after another which rolled over into 2012. God allowed me to be without work from January 2011 to April 2011. I applied at various places but no one hired me. That was the first time in my ten years of being a nurse that I could not find a job within a week from leaving a job. God was testing my faith and taking me through another emotional trial. I cried out day and night for God to raise me up off my back and bed of affliction so I could find a job to move me and my kids into our own place, due to disrespectful things in me and my kids view at the present residence. Finally God answered my prayers and blessed me with a job at a drug rehab.

Soon after that I found a place for me and my kids. I also started to receive employment. So it seemed like things were starting to look brighter. One day I was driving down the road in my car and grieving because of the first God ordained marriage that did not physically take place. As I was grieving, I began to thank God and I stated "God, I know you have my tall, dark, handsome, and bowlegged husband out there." I was just speaking out loud to God while I was grieving because the first did not work. So like a day or so after that I was listening to the Christian radio like I normally do every morning while taking my kids to school. Then this particular message on grieving by this person I did not know caught my attention. I had heard this person before but never paid attention to the person then, but the message was about grieving. I think I had heard the person minister about two times before. I was riding back home in my car. The message about grieving caught my attention even more. So when I got to my driveway the Holy Spirit spoke to me and told me to look up this church. Then I said to myself that that church is in a negative city where violence is and I never want to go there. The church and the person was an hour away where I was reluctant to drive. So I finally listened to the end of the message to see exactly where the church was located and then I wrote down the address. So when I got in my house, I looked up the church on the internet something I had never done before and would not have done if the Holy Spirit would not have told me to do. So when I located the church on the internet, I saw the pastor of the church, and lo and behold it was that tall, dark, bowlegged man that I was just telling God

I know he had for me. God had let me know he had created this person for me because God promised me my desires a long time ago. So I got excited and God through me decided to go visit the church an hour away in another city. So when I got there that Sunday, God put me right in the front of this man while he was preaching. It was like a Ruth gleaning in Boaz's field, just like God sent Ruth to Boaz. I noticed that they noticed me soon as they got behind the podium. They looked at me for a while and then proceeded to speak. I also noticed one lady from his entourage was continuously staring at me. He had an entourage of women surrounding him and I soon found out why later. So as I continued to go there he started to throw a few hints portraying that he knew I was sent by God, because he could see in the spirit also. God revealed that to me and something he said in the air let me know he was spying on me in the spirit realm 'cause that was the only way he could know about what was going on in my life, and I never talked to him physically. He also mentioned things in the air about me joining the church. I prayed about it and since I knew God had led me there that it was okay to join. So my kids and I joined the church, and not long after I joined the church I started seeing and dreaming fleshy (darkness) things about him. The first maybe three times I came it seemed like he was trying to do right, but of course he allowed the devil through immoral women to come between and take his attention completely off God first, then me next, and from then on every time I came I had to watch him be disrespectful and lusting for women in tight clothing. One particular one who would try her hardest to get his attention until she finally got it. So as I would travel back and forth dealing with the pain, hurt, and betrayal and waiting on God to straighten things out with us, so I thought, but I eventually realized much later that, that was not going to be. Because even though that was his will, the Bible states in Amos 3:3, "Can two walk together except they be agreed." So, in other words, two have to accept God's will in order for it to work. He would pretend that he was on my side and even had me fooled. He would voice things in the open like "this one will work" misleading and deceiving lies and phrases. One month after I started going there, I ended up losing my car due to me getting behind in the payments because I was out of work for those months after the job loss.

So I eventually had to move out of my apartment and my kids and I ended up moving back to Florida where we were originally. We ended up going back because I was considering letting my kids stay with their fathers. My plan was to take them to Florida then drive a rental car back to Louisiana, live with my old roommate again. The plan did not work out that way. My kids' fathers both switched out. As soon as the kids and I made it to Tallahassee, one of the fathers did not give the money he promised and the other who was my ex-husband threatened to bother the child support if my son stayed with him and not with me. So my kids and I ended up going to my mother's house.

We were stuck in Tallahassee for three days before we made it to my mother's house. We were out of money due to my daughter's father switching out and not giving me the money he promised for my daughter. We were stuck at a rest area for hours and I prayed and asked God to help us. I ended up calling a shelter as no one in my family would help us and the lady at the shelter helped us. God, through her, rented us a motel room for one night, because the shelter was full, and then she put it on the radio that my kids and I needed a family to sponsor us for two days and God opened up this door with a nice family to take us in for two days.

People who heard on the radio about my kids and I being stranded in Tallahassee gave donations to help us. The lady at the shelter and her assistant gave us some of the donated money to leave Tallahassee and make it to my mother's house five hours away. My mother was not too thrilled about us staying there because she and I were not, and still, are not that close. My oldest sister who would not even send us any money to help us when we were stuck in Tallahassee wanted us to stay with her, but I refused because I knew her and my mother constantly talked about each other, and I did not want to be between them and be expected to take sides. Even though my sister did not send us money to help us, she stated she was praying for us. While at my mother's house I would lock myself in my brother's room when he would go to work because I did not want to be involved in the chaos my family had going on, because I was down there not by choice, but by God's will. Because God chose me and because of the anointing God has placed on my life, I had to suffer for it. The Bible states in Matthew 22:14, "For many are called, but few are chosen." It also states in Luke 12:48, "For unto whomsoever much is given, of him shall be much required." So as I stated it was not by choice, but by God's will that is why I had to go through all of the hard things I went through including these next ones.

Because the ministry of women that God placed inside of me had to be brought out, and even though all the hurts, disappointments, rejection, betrayal, etc., did not feel good, but it was for my good and for God's glory. While down at my mom's house after a few weeks, problems began to arise. It seemed like no matter how I tried to lock myself in my brother's room to avoid issues, the devil proceeded to bother me anyway. My mom and I ended up getting into a dispute over a chair that I wanted to take outside and use. She made a big deal over the chair, because she would pretty nitpick over everything I did, even if I cooked that was an issue. While my mom and I debated over the chair, my oldest sister was over there. She interfered between my mom and me because she was already upset because I did not want to stay with her. She and I soon started to argue with each other. She then got up in my face and wanted to do me harm. So I then grabbed a weapon because she was twice my size. She then went outside and called our cousin who is a pastor/prophet; the same cousin who prophesized to me before all this was going on. When I was in Louisiana and told me the devil was trying to take me out emotionally.

So when she called our cousin which was her friend also due to them being the same age, my sister put the speaker phone on and began to laugh at me because I was upset and arguing and stating to her and my mom, "Christians like y'all make a person not want to be a Christian."

She was attempting to laugh at me, to scorn and mock me, and she thought my cousin was going to be a participant but she was not. My cousin stated to my sister to give me the phone and when my sister gave me the phone, my cousin told me to go in the back. My cousin then stated to me that God was dealing with her concerning me while on her bed and that he showed her how the devil was trying to bother me and I do not have to even open my mouth; and that is exactly what was happening. The devil was attempting to make me his bull's-eye without success. After my sister was eavesdropping on me and my cousin's phone conversation and she heard my cousin taking the right side (my side) and not her side because she was wrong, finally she took her phone from me. My cousin told me really fast to call her on my phone before my sister took her phone. So I called my cousin on my phone and my sister got upset and she went to her house. About days after that my mom started really acting funny and called my oldest sister on the phone, and I overheard her telling my sister she wanted to come to her house until I left. So she ended up going to my sister's house that day and that night she or my sister called the police on me for no reason and sent them to her house where my kids and I were. They told the police untrue things because when the police came they asked me if I tried to hurt myself. I told the police I had no clue what they were talking about and I even thought they were there to see my brothers and not myself because I did not do anything and do not get in trouble. My brothers did not either, so of course I was really wondering why they were there and who called them.

God revealed to me who it was that called them but nothing became of it. It hurt me and caused me to have a miniature breakdown, but God helped me through it. After that incident my kids and I were stranded down there at my mom's house a few more weeks while my mom remained at my sister's house, and none of them, just only my two brothers talking to me and my kids the remainder of the time we were down there. God finally opened up a door sooner than expected concerning me getting one of my sisters' help. She helped me get a car by putting it in her name. God also opened up doors for job interviews back in Louisiana. I could not work in Florida at that time because I was living in Louisiana for six years. After I managed to get another car with God's help first, then my sister's help next, I still was undecided about what I was going to do. I really was reluctant about going back to Louisiana because I felt if the man I mentioned earlier that God created for me cared about me, he would have found me. So I really did not care about going back there, I was really considering Miami where the sister that helped me get the car lived. Then while still in Florida one Sunday while I was in church, God, through the pastor, told me that there was something God was telling me to do but I was reluctant to do it and that I needed to obey God. I know what she was talking about and it was concerning me moving back to Louisiana, something I did not really feel like doing because of personal reasons. So I obeyed God and my kids and I packed up everything in the car and left early one morning. No one said good bye. Only my brothers were speaking to us—not my mom or sister.

I talked to my old roommate prior to us leaving and they stated we could come and live again with them. God through me drove all the way from Florida back to Louisiana still in shock and wounded by family. When my kids and I got to Louisiana in Baton Rouge, I called my roommate. They stated they were on their way to their house but they never made it there any time soon. So my kids and I sat out in the car piled with clothing, etc. and waited and waited. I attempted to call them again but they texted one time with an attitude and told me they were coming and soon they completely stopped answering their phone and responding, so they left us high and dry. I then took the last forty dollars I had and my kids and I went to the Red Roof Inn. After we took our things up there I told my kids that I was going to go to church that Wednesday night. I wanted to see if the man God created for me even cared or had changed and surrendered to God. He knew what I had been through because as I stated earlier God had already revealed to me that he was spying on me in the spirit realm before I left Baton Rouge. So when I got to his church I was hit with another sharp blow. He had the very same one that was trying her hardest to get his attention when she was in the audience. He had that very one now working for him as a security officer following him around in the church with a big smile on her face. Then after that every Sunday and Wednesday she would be sitting in the front almost by him pretending to be a security officer but really one of his girlfriends. Just imagine how I felt that Wednesday, after I had been through everything else. So the next day which was that Thursday, my kids and I had to leave the motel. I attempted to contact again my old roommate but still they did not respond. So I called around to shelters in Baton Rouge. With no success, I then called shelters in New Orleans and one let me and my kids in right away.

About thirty minutes into our drive to the shelter in New Orleans my old roommate called. They stated that they dropped their phone in the toilet the night before. While on the phone, God just told me to keep going to New Orleans to the shelter and not to turn back.

When we got to the shelter we were asked questions by the director then they took us to our room which was an adjoining room. It was what I needed at that time, because I was still in shock. My kids slept on one side and I was on the other with the door closed. I was having issues due to the shock and everybody I heard outside of the room door sounded like they were in a tunnel talking. Days later, after the shock wore off the people's voices started to sound louder. I also caught the flu the same day we came and I slept it off that entire weekend. That Monday I went to look for a job and soon found one at a hospice. I still continued going to that church in spite the negative things the person who, once again was supposed to be for me, was doing to the female who would continuously look at me with evil looks. The man knew about it but did not care because eventually God revealed to me that he was really on her side, not mine because darkness does not like light and that is what I was, and he or she was not. God also revealed to me that the man was dealing in witchcraft. I dreamed that while I was sitting in his church, he would be walking by me and waving a tarot sign (something like a tarot card). The purpose of him doing this was to work witchcraft on me to make me fall in love him, which didn't work. I did not think much into the dream because the man would spy on me in the spirit and I did not want to start anything with him, and then I thought that maybe he practiced witchcraft before he became a Christian. I guess I was trying to give him the benefit of the doubt only for it to blow up in my face later. I came back up to Louisiana in October 2011 and I sat there in that church being disrespected, deceived, and hurt; might as well say cheated on also because once again the person God showed me that was for me, they desired whoremongering women in tight clothing and rejected me—the real Christian who was not trying to sleep with them and wear nasty clothing to get their attention and seduce them, and they both fail for the women sent by the devil to get these so called pastors out of God's will, and the women succeeded. January 2012 the man at that church decided that they wanted to put me out of that church for no reason, because they were really evil and did not want to surrender to God and do it God's way, but they wanted to continue operating in witchcraft, fornication, etc., and do it their way. God had already told me through this true woman of God at another church that I need to be around the real anointing, but I still did not leave there from his church because I thought that if I came to the prayer services and prayed with them and everyone else, I thought that prayer would change him, but it did not because he did not want the change. So as I stated earlier in January, one Wednesday prayer service he had his administration put me out of the church because he was evil.

So after he put me out I got spiritually sick and had to drop down from working a full-time job and go to part-time work. Mainly on every Wednesday night while I would be at work or home, my spirit would get so vexed and disturbed for some reason. I am assuming that is mainly when he would sleep around with whoever he picked up from the fake church service that Wednesday night, because later on God let me have a dream that it was a bed in the front of his church and I saw in the dream the back of him having sex with someone. After a few months passed, around March the same year, I started feeling better and I would go out on the streets of New Orleans and minister to people who did not know God. I began to do that when I was not working to keep my mind off the bad things he did to me. Then one night I was lying on my couch and I felt something molesting then raping me. God automatically showed in the spirit that it was him sending out witchcraft spirits seducing spirits. I began then to plead the blood of Jesus over and over again and try to fight it. He tortured me off and on all night with these violating seducing spirits. I was so tired the next day until I could not go to work that day. I called my spiritual father in Florida the next day and told him about it, and I also called other pastors to start a prayer chain. After they prayed, it felt that he stopped and it began to fade. Then it was like I literally felt him pushing his way back in. God gave these words to me when I was on my bed crying out to God, "The devil can afflict your body but he cannot touch your soul." The same words he told the devil concerning Job when God allowed the devil to afflict Job just how he allowed the devil to lightly afflict me, but not touch my soul. God's word states in Psalm 34:19, "Many are the afflictions of the righteous, but the Lord delivereth him out of the all." The afflictions eventually lightened up so eventually God was and still is dealing with and touching my enemy for touching me, because he also states in his word Psalm 105:15, "Touch not mine anointed, and do my prophets no harm." So in other words, God allowed me to encounter afflictions, rejection, hurt, and pain, betrayal, deception, etc., to obtain blessings, a great anointing, strength, closeness with God, elevation and promotion, and to continue being his eagle, his qualified, a vessel unto honor and much more for God's glory.

www.ingramcontent.com/pod-product-compliance
Lightning Source LLC
Chambersburg PA
CBHW071025040426
42443CB00007B/931